CALLED & GIFTED

FOR THE

Third Millennium

Reflections of the U.S. Catholic Bishops on the
Thirtieth Anniversary of the *Decree on the Apostolate of the Laity*
and the Fifteenth Anniversary of *Called and Gifted*

"[The Lord] sends them on the Church's apostolate,

an apostolate that is one yet has different forms and methods,

an apostolate that must all the time be adapting itself

to the needs of the moment. . . ."

Decree on the Apostolate of the Laity (no. 33)

Called and Gifted for the Third Millennium was developed by the Committee on the Laity. It was approved by the Administrative Committee in September 1995 and by the membership of the National Conference of Catholic Bishops at their general meeting in November 1995. *Called and Gifted for the Third Millennium* is authorized for publication by the undersigned.

Monsignor Dennis M. Schnurr
General Secretary
NCCB/USCC

In 2001 the National Conference of Catholic Bishops and United States Catholic Conference became the United States Conference of Catholic Bishops.

Scriptural texts used in this work are taken from the *New American Bible*, copyright © 1991, 1986, and 1970 by the Confraternity of Christian Doctrine, and are used with permission of the copyright holder. All rights reserved.

Cover images: *iStockphoto.com*.

ISBN 978-1-57455-002-3

First Printing, December 1995
Eighth Printing, March 2013

Contents

A Prayer

God of love and mercy, you call us to be your people,

you gift us with your abundant grace.

Make us a holy people, radiating the fullness of your love.

Form us into a community, a people who care,
expressing your compassion.

Remind us day after day of our baptismal call to serve,
with joy and courage.

Teach us how to grow in wisdom and grace and joy
in your presence.

Through Jesus and in your Spirit, we make this prayer.

Introduction

What is the Spirit saying to the world today through the Church in the United States, particularly through the lives of lay men and women?

In 1980 we bishops listened to the message of that same Holy Spirit. In our pastoral statement *Called and Gifted*, we acknowledged and reflected upon the ways lay men and women were answering the Lord's call and employing their gifts to take an active and responsible part in the mission of the Church.

Now, fifteen years after *Called and Gifted*, we take that statement's four "calls"—to holiness, to community, to mission and ministry, and to adulthood/Christian maturity—and update them in light of Church teaching, pastoral practice, and changing conditions in the world. We also identify several challenges and suggest questions for individual and group reflection.

In *Called and Gifted* we addressed the whole Church but focused on the laity, inviting them to respond with "next words." In consultation, structured dialogue, correspondence, and reports, they did so with honesty and integrity.

Now, with the benefit of fifteen additional years of consulting the laity, we again address the whole Church, with a focus on the vocation and mission of lay persons. Moreover, we invite all members of the Church—lay men and women in secular life or consecrated life and the ordained—to continue the dialogue with one another and with us.

In this statement we look back with gratitude upon the Second Vatican Council and prepare in hope for the third millennium. We believe that the Church's path into a new millennium is marked by a faithful listening to the Spirit in the midst of God's people.

The Call to Holiness

*Life according to the Spirit, whose fruit is holiness (cf. Rom 6:22; Gal 5:22)
stirs up every baptized person and requires each to follow and imitate Jesus Christ,
in embracing the beatitudes, in listening and meditating on the Word of God,
in conscious and active participation in the liturgical and sacramental life of the
Church, in personal prayer, in family or in community, in the hunger and thirst for
justice, in the practice of the commandment of love in all circumstances of life and
service to the brethren, especially the least, the poor and the suffering.*
(*Christifideles Laici*, no. 16)

The Witness of Holy Lives

During the last fifteen years, the Christian lay faithful have contributed greatly to
the spiritual heritage of the Church, enlarging our understanding of what it means to
be called to holiness, that is, to be called to "ever more intimate union with Christ"
(*Catechism of the Catholic Church*, no. 2014). Their union with Christ is evident in a
deepened awareness of the spiritual dimensions of life.

St. Paul wrote to his friend, co-worker, and co-disciple St. Timothy that the value
of spirituality is immeasurable because it holds promise for our present life and life
hereafter (see 1 Tm 4:8).

We have heard the testimony of many lay persons who have discovered the wisdom
of St. Paul's words and who understand that we all share in the one vocation to holiness.
They know in their hearts the teaching of the Second Vatican Council: "The forms and
tasks of life are many, but holiness is one—that sanctity which is cultivated by all who
act under God's Spirit" (*Lumen Gentium*, no. 41).

While spirituality is more and more an explicit aspect of Christian life, "spiritual
sight" or insight is not sufficient in itself. The call to holiness requires effort and commitment to live the beatitudes. We have seen this active spirituality in the lives of
countless lay persons and have listened to their stories.

How one experiences the challenges and joys of life in the Spirit is deeply shaped
by the concrete realities of one's life. The most frequently mentioned place where
lay people encounter Christ is in Christian marriage and family life. We believe that
Christian marriage is vocation, sacrament, covenant relationship, and mission. In the
sacrament of marriage Christ is made present in a special way to spouses, family members, and the overall society. The Christian family is a sign and means of unity and
solidarity in our world. The intimacy of marriage, parents' all encompassing care of

children, the struggle of single–parent families, single persons' relationships with their family members and friends, the battle with addictions, the challenges of caring for aging family members with dignity and love, the acceptance of loss—these are recognized as means of grace.

The laity also speak of the parish as a place where they experience the living God. In the sacraments (especially the Eucharist), in counseling and spiritual guidance, and in study and prayer groups, people come to know the power of the Spirit. Some have described being away from the Church for years, and one day crossing the threshold of a parish in search of "something" they can't always identify. There they find Christ's love visible in worship, in the sacrament of reconciliation, in a caring community, and in service to the poor. And they are encouraged to return, again and again.

In their work—teaching, cosmetology, medicine, the arts, house painting, real estate—laity discover both meaning and a sense of mission, relating their work to their spiritual life. Their work paths, no matter how diverse, often help them to move beyond self-absorption toward active caring for others.

> **"The laity's call to holiness is a gift from the Holy Spirit. Their response is a gift to the Church and to the world."**

For lay persons of all ages, nature reveals the wonder of God. Older people confined to their homes meditate on the changing seasons; they see that God makes all things new (see Rv 21:5). Children observe the ways of nature and the universe and see the Creator at work. Youth are moved to care for the environment and to set an example of stewardship. Prayers of praise rise from these men, women, and children, echoing the psalmist: "Let the rivers clap their hands, the mountains shout with them for joy" (Ps 98:8).

A common thread in the laity's accounts of their spiritual lives is the primacy of relationships. The bonds of family and friendship, of neighborhood and parish are vital to lay women and men. These relationships help them form ever deeper bonds of unity with Jesus Christ.

Formed in Suffering

Often people can go the extra mile for others because they have been spiritually formed through suffering. For Christians, suffering is both hope and challenge.

St. Paul writes: "We know that affliction makes for endurance, and endurance for tested virtue, and tested virtue for hope" (Rom 5:3-4). The laity of our Church are moved to act on behalf of those in need because they have come to know Christ in the depths of their own suffering. Some have been betrayed by their marriage partners. Others, many of whom are women, have endured physical and emotional abuse. Children have had to adjust to divorced and separated parents. And parents have known helplessness as their children leave the Church, become addicted to drugs, or accept an ethic of casual sex. Others have experienced prejudice or discrimination because of their language or racial background. As people have lost their jobs, their homes, or their loved ones, they have also found the abundance of God's mercy; they know the hope of which St. Paul speaks.

In the darkness that surrounds them, they discover the light of Christ and the truth that "The way of perfection passes by way of the Cross" (*Catechism of the Catholic Church*, no. 2015). They are ready to help others along the way and in so doing become signs of hope.

As we enter the third millennium, we may well see more collective suffering. As Americans, we tend to believe that effective planning can reduce, or even eliminate, certain kinds of suffering. Experience sometimes points to the contrary. New strains of disease, persistent economic instability, large movements of displaced persons, and a multiplicity of wars are already a reality and may increase. On a smaller scale, civil discourse is quickly disappearing while calumny and detraction are on the rise. Too often, angry words, sometimes rooted in prejudice, lead to violent acts, shattering whole communities.

How can the Church meet such challenges with realistic hope? Church leaders can continue to speak out and to take action against social injustice, which is the cause of so much suffering. Another way is for the entire Church, especially its leaders, both ordained and lay, to recognize our own implication in the suffering of others and to ask for forgiveness when that is required. In preparation for the third millennium, our Holy Father has set an example by calling the Church to repent of "past errors and instances of infidelity, inconsistency and slowness to act" (*Tertio Millennio Adveniente*, no. 33). We bishops seek to follow his example.

The witness of the laity also gives hope. Their presence within the web of society can be a source of solace and strength in the face of enormous human need. The laity are "the front lines of the Church's life . . . they ought to have an ever clearer consciousness not only of belonging to the Church, but of being the Church . . . that is to say, the community of the faithful on earth under the leadership of the Pope, the common head, and of the bishops in communion with him. They are the Church" (*Christifideles Laici*, no. 9, quoted in *Catechism of the Catholic Church*, no. 899).

Beyond acts of holy compassion—blessed as they are—the laity are called to confront unjust elements in various social systems. They are called by God to apply Christian principles to government, medical research, social services, education, the media—in short, to all those human institutions that exist to help human persons realize their inherent dignity.

For Generous Service

Generosity is surely a sign of holiness. During the past fifteen years, thousands of lay men and women have given generously of their time and energy in a variety of ways. Their service in domestic and foreign missions is particularly notable. We rejoice especially in the large number of young adults who devote one or more years to Church or public service. Their stories of selfless compassion stand in sharp contrast to prevalent images of private achievement and acquisition. Their stories are living examples of responding to the Holy Father's call for young people to be signs of hope. They are not caught up in materialism, as some charge the young are, but are coming to know that Christ shows himself in a special way in the poor and in the vulnerable.

While not everyone may be called to this exact form of service, we all—clergy and laity alike—can be motivated by such example to examine our daily behavior and choices about what we buy, what entertainment and recreation we choose, and what other comforts we seek—in short, how we use our material resources.

In Simplicity of Life

The human family is facing major choices regarding lifestyle. As economic and ecological issues are increasingly intertwined, we see more clearly that the earth's resources are not limitless. Industrialized nations consume more and more of what God created for all to enjoy, while developing nations can scarcely support their populations.

What is to be done? Biblical teachings about the essential goodness of creation, the human person's responsibility for the stewardship of God's gifts, and the thoroughly changed heart are important resources to draw upon as we try to establish an economy that is just, sustainable, and ecologically responsible. In addition, the Church's tradition of simplicity, embodied in the original charisms of religious orders, merits serious reflection and dialogue as a means of addressing the imbalance.

Challenges for the Future

Because the laity's call to holiness is a vocation in every sense of the word, it makes demands and poses challenges. Many challenges are embedded in the call to holiness on this eve of a new era, but we have raised up three as particularly apt for our time: (1) to make an explicit connection between holiness and active service, especially to the poor and vulnerable; (2) to recognize that human suffering—so much a part of the laity's life—can be the catalyst for them to carry forth the Church's healing ministry in diverse ways; (3) to reappropriate the Church's tradition of a simple lifestyle in light of the pressing need for justice, as well as preserving the earth for ourselves and for generations to come.

The laity's call to holiness is a gift from the Holy Spirit. Their response is a gift to the Church and to the world.

Discussion Questions

1. In what ways do you believe you "know" God in ordinary life?
2. Do you believe you are called to care for some segment of human need? What is it?
3. How does your own life experience, including suffering, equip you to carry on Christ's healing ministry?
4. What changes are needed to live more simply in your home? in the Church? in the nation?

The Call to Community

From the communion that Christians experience in Christ there immediately flows the communion which they experience with one another: all are branches of a single vine, namely, Christ.
(*Christifideles Laici*, no. 18)

Christian Community in Family and Parish

The renewed outpouring of the Spirit of Pentecost in our times has stimulated a great desire for experiences of deeper Christian community. This was true when we issued *Called and Gifted* in 1980 and it has become even more obvious in the years since then. We note, for example, the growth of faith-sharing groups, study and support groups, lay associations and movements, as well as the increasing number of lay persons joining secular institutes, pious associations, and third orders.

Above all, people long for community in their families and in their parishes. Both are basic and essential to living a fully Christian life. Both communities—the domestic church and the parish church—are challenged: to live faithfully, particularly when changes occur upsetting comfortable patterns; to be life-giving by welcoming and caring for children and by reaching out in service to the needy; and to grow in mutuality, i.e., the realization of our equality as persons created in God's image. By living with these challenges and humbly engaging them, vital Christian communities can be forged.

Beyond the intimate community of family life, the parish is for most Catholics their foremost experience of Christian community, enabling them to express their faith, grow in unity with God and others, and continue the saving mission of Christ. We have seen a welcome renewal in all aspects of parish life and ministry, due in large measure to an informed and committed laity often encouraged by their pastors and priests imbued with the spirit of Vatican II. In addition, the increase of people from different racial and ethnic cultures has been challenging parishes, dioceses, and communities not only to spread a larger, more welcoming table, but also to learn how diversity builds up the Body of Christ. African American congregations have discovered much of their worship heritage and have enriched Catholic liturgical life. "All of us have been given to drink of the one Spirit. Now the body is not one member, it is many" (1 Cor 12:13-14).

Small Communities of Faith

A new and promising development, often occurring in the context of parish renewal, has been the formation of small church communities which testify to "the creative grace of God at work" and are "a source of great hope for the whole Church" (*Communion and Mission*, p. 1). The mobility of our population, the stresses of the society in which we live, and often the size of parishes are factors leading people to want to participate in the Church's life and ministry on a smaller scale.

Small church communities take shape in various ways. Sometimes people are drawn to them through a parish renewal process or through one of the lay movements and associations, which often provide for their members the experience of Christian community. The Rite of Christian Initiation of Adults (RCIA) can lead members of a parish to become a small community which invites and catechizes those who are considering joining the Church. Still other small communities are organized in neighborhoods or are rooted in various natural groupings that may exist within a parish.

Small church communities not only foster the faith of individuals; they are living cells that build up the Body of Christ. They are to be signs and instruments of unity. As basic units of the parish, they serve to increase the corporate life and mission of the parish by sharing in its life generously with their talents and support.

Drawing upon the thorough discussion of small communities that took place at the 1987 synod on the vocation and mission of the lay faithful, Pope John Paul II has urged local ecclesiastical authorities to foster these "living" communities, for they are "where the faithful can communicate the Word of God and express it in service and love to one another; these communities are true expressions of ecclesial communion and centers of evangelization, in communion with their pastors" (*Christifideles Laici*, no. 26).

In all cases, authentic small Christian communities are characterized by obedience to the word of God, common prayer, a commitment of time to one another for building personal relationships, meaningful participation in the life of their local parish, some form of apostolic mission to the wider society, an adherence to the Catholic faith, and an explicit relationship of communion with the Church.

The growing Hispanic/Latino and Asian presence in our country, as well as the influence of other ethnic groups, has been a creative impetus in the formation of small Christian communities. As our Church becomes increasingly multicultural, these small communities can enable lay people from different backgrounds to come to know one another in a trusting way, creating bonds of solidarity, a commitment to mission, and new lay leaders.

Challenges for the Future

(1) Pastoral leaders should feel challenged to serve the laity by helping them develop and sustain small Christian communities—including those based on careers and professions. Laity, too, should take a leadership role, working with their pastors to develop these faith communities, bringing their own gifts and wisdom acquired from family and work to renew our Church. In no case, however, should small church communities forget their rootedness in the family—the first and most basic form of the Church—or sever their links to the larger faith community present in the parish and diocese.

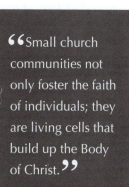

66Small church communities not only foster the faith of individuals; they are living cells that build up the Body of Christ.**99**

(2) The laity are called to participate in a "new evangelization." This means sharing the good news of Jesus personally through the witness of our lives. Moreover, the new evangelization is "directed not only to persons but also to entire portions of populations in the variety of their situations, surroundings and cultures" (*Christifideles Laici,* no. 34). Its purpose is to challenge, through the power of the Gospel, those values, judgments, patterns of behavior, sources of inspiration, and models of life that are inconsistent with the word of God and the plan of salvation (cf. *Evangelii Nuntiandi,* no. 19) and to affirm the ways God is working in the world today.

(3) Small church communities offer an important and unique means of formation for the new evangelization. They strengthen their members to persevere in their faith and mission, providing both inspiration and practical support. To be involved in the new evangelization, however, requires that members of such communities be as ready for engagement with the world outside their community as they are for deepening their relationships within it. If the small community is to be a true expression of the mystery of the Church,

then it must be "a communion of God's people living out the mission of Jesus Christ in the power of the Spirit" (*Communion and Mission*, p. 8).

Discussion Questions

1. What are the most important elements of parish life that foster community for you as a lay person? What do you need from your parish? What can/should you contribute to your parish—time, talent, treasure?
2. What experience of Christian community have you had (e.g., Cursillo, Christian Family Movement, Bible study, Focolare, RENEW, the charismatic renewal)? How valuable for your Christian growth is the small community?
3. How do the small church communities you know relate to the parish? How are they connected to the family?
4. How do you think small Christian communities can help the laity participate in a "new evangelization"?

The Call to Mission and Ministry

The ministries which exist and are at work at this time in the Church are all, even in their variety of forms, a participation in Jesus Christ's own ministry as the Good Shepherd who lays down his life for the sheep, the humble servant who gives himself without reserve for the salvation of all.
(*Christifideles Laici*, no. 21)

Participation in the Church's Life and Mission as the Sacrament of Christ in the World

Through the sacraments of Baptism, Confirmation, and Eucharist every Christian is called to participate actively and co-responsibly in the Church's mission of salvation in the world. Moreover, in those same sacraments, the Holy Spirit pours out gifts that make it possible for every Christian man and woman to assume different ministries and forms of service that complement one another and are for the good of all (cf. *Christifideles Laici*, no. 20).

Everyone has a responsibility to answer the call to mission and to develop the gifts she or he has been given by sharing them in the family, the workplace, the civic community, and the parish or diocese. A parallel responsibility exists within the Church's leadership "to acknowledge and foster the ministries, the offices, and the roles of the lay faithful that find their foundation in the sacraments of baptism and confirmation, indeed, for a good many of them in the sacrament of matrimony" (*Christifideles Laici*, no. 23).

The Holy Father teaches that any ministries, offices, and roles undertaken by lay persons are to be exercised "in conformity to their specific lay vocation" (*Christifideles Laici*, no. 23). This, according to the Second Vatican Council, is that "the laity . . . make the Church present and operative in those places and circumstances where only through them can she become the salt of the earth" (*Lumen Gentium*, no. 33). A striking example is found in family life where, according to Pope John Paul II, the work "of evangelization carried out by Christian parents is original and irreplaceable" (*Familiaris Consortio*, no. 53).

Today Christian Churches must communicate the importance of the laity's witness and service within the family and within the professional, social, political, and cultural life of society. An effective parish or congregation will help its members make the connections between worship and work, between liturgy and life in the family, community, and workplace. For this reason, church ministers—especially clergy—are called to strengthen and equip lay people to be witnesses to Christ, acting in the power of him who is the Good Shepherd and humble servant of all. We can make common cause with all Christian Churches around this endeavor.

Lay Ministry in the Church

When *Called and Gifted* was published, we were just beginning to experience the tide of professionally prepared lay men and women offering their talents and charisms in the service of the Church. These persons are often called ecclesial lay ministers.

Over the past fifteen years, we have seen great numbers of lay people become involved in the liturgy as cantors and music directors, readers, Eucharistic ministers, and altar servers. Furthermore, in some places laity are responsible for leading Sunday worship in the absence of a priest. Men and women of all ages engage in these ministries, which in turn can be a means of spiritual and religious formation for them. As people study the Scriptures that they will proclaim, coordinate musical texts with liturgical seasons, or study eucharistic theology, they are touched in mind and spirit. Being steeped in word and sacrament is a classic means of transforming the human spirit; the grace of this moment is the transformation of so many laity.

The lay faithful are engaged in ministries of other kinds that are also formative. They share the faith of the Church through teaching young people as well as adults; they serve in peace and justice networks, in soup kitchens and shelters, in marriage preparation, in bereavement programs, and in ministry to the separated and divorced. All these actions, when performed in the name of Jesus and enacted under the aegis of the Church, are forms of ministry. Recent research indicates that at least half of our parishes have lay people or vowed religious in pastoral staff positions. In some instances the daily pastoral leadership of a parish has been entrusted to a lay person, in the absence of a resident pastor. Indeed, the pastoral needs of this moment are being ably and generously served by many kinds of ecclesial lay ministers.

Lay ministry is a reality beyond the parish as well. Many church institutions, from colleges and school systems to marriage tribunals, from social services and health care providers to houses of formation, benefit from the expertise and dedication of Catholic women and men exercising their designated ministry.

The Church's mission is being carried forward and far by all these lay ministers who tirelessly serve the Church and God's people. We join pastors and parishioners in expressing gratitude for this development.

Ecclesial lay ministers speak of their work, their service, as a calling, not merely a job. They believe God has called them to their ministry, and often the parish priest is the means of discerning the call.

Challenges for the Future

We, and all pastoral leaders, feel challenged:

1. To develop and commit the resources necessary to help laity, both paid staff and volunteers, prepare for church ministry. Lay ministers have often invested in their own education and preparation for ministry and they need Church support.

2. To practice justice in the workplace and to provide a living wage. It is often difficult for lay ministers to support themselves and their families.

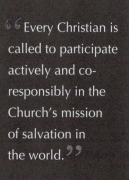

" Every Christian is called to participate actively and co-responsibly in the Church's mission of salvation in the world. "

3. To incorporate minority lay ministers into ecclesial leadership.

4. To ensure that the Church becomes an exemplary steward of all its human resources. With the entire Church we give thanks that the Church has been blessed with many laity who feel called to ecclesial ministry, even as we continue to work and pray for vocations to the priesthood, diaconate, and consecrated life. We also recognize that God is blessing the Church with lay vocations to ministry.

Finally, we urge Catholic laity to bring Christ's peace and justice to the world by working energetically to reclaim national concern for the common good.

One challenge undergirds all of the above. It is the need to foster respectful collaboration, leading to mutual support in ministry, between clergy and laity for the sake of Christ's Church and its mission to the world. This is a huge task requiring changes in patterns of reflection, behavior, and expectation among laity and clergy alike. As an episcopal conference, we will expand our study and dialogue concerning lay ministry in order to understand better the critical issues and find effective ways to address them. The new evangelization will become a reality only if ordained and lay members of Christ's faithful understand their roles and ministries as complementary, and their purposes joined to the one mission and ministry of Jesus Christ. His prayer at the Last Supper must be our prayer, "That all may be one." Collaboration in ministry is a way to realize that unity.

Discussion Questions

1. When have you really felt ministered to? From this experience, what conclusions would you draw about the meaning and purpose of ministry?
2. In what areas of your life are you responding to the call to ministry? What help from the Church do you need in pursuing your call?
3. In what ways could ordained and lay ministers collaborate more effectively and offer mutual support in ministry?
4. In what ways are you, as an adult, continuing to be educated and formed in the Catholic faith?

The Call to Christian Maturity

*The gospel image of the vine and the branches reveals to us another
fundamental aspect of the lay faithful's life and mission: the call to growth
and a continual process of maturation, of always bearing much fruit.*
(Christifideles Laici, no. 57)

Holiness, community, and ministry are facets of Christian life that come to
full expression only by means of development and growth toward Christian
maturity. This fourth call of our reflection on the laity is, in its entirety, a major
challenge as the Church enters the new millennium. For the laity, the challenge
is woven throughout the "web of their existence" (*Lumen Gentium*, no. 31).

Certainly the ordinary dynamics of life—caring for a family, job responsibilities, exercising the duties of citizenship—demand growth in maturity. But
we draw particular attention to certain attitudes and behaviors that signal
new levels of maturity needed among Catholic lay men and women in the
third millennium.

Caring for Children

Mature persons actively care for future generations. Christian maturity
requires that all of us, lay and ordained, provide the best catechesis possible
for children and youth. In the past we have pledged our support to parents
and families as they seek to undertake their responsibility as primary educa-
tors of their children. We renew that pledge. The revitalization of youth ministry, which has been taking place since Pope John Paul II's visit to Denver
and World Youth Day in 1993, is a marvelous sign of how adults can care for
young people.

We realize, though, that these are troubled and trying times and many
children lack the stable presence of family. The Church's social teaching
regarding the common good suggests the need for all adults to become conscious of their responsibilities for the young people who are part of their worlds,
especially the disabled and the unborn who are among the most vulnerable.

Mature persons of faith can foster the natural resilience in children and
youth who live in stressful circumstances. A grandparent, an older sibling, a
teacher, librarian, coach, or neighbor—each one can take the time to listen
to a child or to a youth and to stir up hope in them. It is often these informal

but compassionate contacts that help children and youth discover meaning in their lives and gain energy to press forward.

A major challenge for the third millennium is to bring our Catholic tradition to life in the hearts, minds, and spirits of new generations. No one does this alone; God's grace is the context and the means. All are called to the task of handing on the faith of our mothers and fathers, of the martyrs and saints.

Religious and Theological Education

In the last fifteen years many of the lay faithful have moved beyond the learning laboratories of ordinary life to more systematic education in theology, Scripture, spiritual life, religious studies, and spiritual direction. This development has been beneficial to growing numbers of lay women and men who, in turn, have helped the whole Church understand and communicate the truths of our faith in new ways.

We urge that theological education and formation be extended to more lay persons. In *Strengthening the Bonds of Peace,* we specifically encouraged women to pursue studies in Scripture, theology, and canon law. Now we similarly encourage lay men, so that the Church—and they themselves—may benefit from these scholarly efforts. Innovative ways must be found to bring the best of the Catholic intellectual and spiritual tradition to more laity. Print and electronic media, computer networks, and mentoring programs offer exciting possibilities. The Church needs a well-educated, inquiring, and vocal laity if the new evangelization is to achieve its full potential.

Respect for Differences

Another sign of Christian maturity is respect for differences. This respect, rooted in humility, understands that unity does not require uniformity. The Catholic tradition welcomes diversity as an enrichment, not a threat. At the same time, we recognize that some differences are rooted in culture and custom while others reside at the level of essential beliefs and teachings. Even at this level, growth and understanding are possible and indeed necessary.

In his encyclical letter *Ut Unum Sint,* the pope rejoices in a renewed awareness of other Christians as "brothers and sisters" instead of "enemies." At this moment in history, when Christian solidarity on behalf of human need is so urgent, a mature Catholic laity will search for common ground with Christians and other people of good will, not stand behind impregnable walls.

We realize that we cannot hold on to this common ground without civility. As we said in *Strengthening the Bonds of Peace*, we must strive for dialogue that is clear, sensitive, patient, and built on trust.

Participation

We consider lay participation in church life at all levels a gift of the Holy Spirit, given for the common good. Laity can and should exercise responsible participation both individually and in groups, not only at the invitation of church leadership but by their own initiative.

Too numerous to mention by name are all those instances in which lay persons have organized educational, advocacy, or charitable efforts that have helped the Church be a more credible and effective witness to the Gospel in public life. In addition, the Church's mission is carried out with creativity and generosity by the many lay movements and associations that have been established for various spiritual and apostolic purposes. These groups play such an essential role in the Christian formation of individuals as well as in the Christian transformation of society that the Church acknowledges and guarantees in law the right of lay persons to form associations (canon 215).

> **66** The Church needs a well-educated, inquiring, and vocal laity if the new evangelization is to achieve its full potential. **99**

We bishops are grateful particularly for the participation of laity in the development of the pastoral letters on peace, on the economy, and in a number of other statements on the family, on women, and on the religious response to violence. Their knowledge and expertise, as well as their constructive inquiry, helped create a mature dialogue with church teaching that enriched our final products. The challenge is to keep that dialogue alive.

The competence of the lay faithful is evident in their participation in the various councils of church governance. The Code of Canon Law requires finance councils in parishes and dioceses. Furthermore, it encourages the establishment of pastoral councils both for dioceses and parishes (canons 511-514, 536-537). Because we believe that they can enrich the life of the Church, we strongly encourage efforts to establish them where they do not exist.

Our conference of bishops benefits from the National Advisory Council, composed mostly of laity, who forward to us their reactions to proposed pastoral documents and other initiatives.

These various councils, at all levels of church leadership, are opportunities for the Church to listen to the wisdom of the laity. So, too, are diocesan synods and pastoral planning processes, which bring together all segments of the Church for mature deliberation about what priorities a diocesan Church should pursue. The challenge is to nurture the growth and development of these various consultative bodies.

We call on all pastoral leaders to strengthen the structures of participation in church life, so that we might listen to one another, grow in understanding, and deepen our experience of dialogue.

Living with Mystery

An embrace of the paschal mystery frees the Christian disciple to live fully despite ambiguity or turmoil. As Christians, we recognize the truth of St. Paul's insight: "Now we see indistinctly, as in a mirror; then we shall see face to face" (1 Cor 13:12). When we embrace our lives, with all their unresolved, mysterious ways, then we are led into the divine embrace of the Mystery that lies at the heart of life. We realize that we are called to be faithful, not necessarily successful. We know that one person might plant the seed, another water it, but God makes it grow (cf. 1 Cor 3:6). It is at this juncture, perhaps more than any other, that the ordained and lay members of the Church can sustain each another in the path of fidelity to Our Lord Jesus Christ.

Offering encouragement is a concrete way of helping someone be faithful to a vocation. The laity and the ordained need to pray for one another and offer mutual support. Furthermore, the Church's pastoral ministry can be more effective if we become true collaborators, mindful of our weaknesses, but grateful for our gifts. Collaboration challenges us to understand that we are, in reality, joined in Christ's body, that we are not separate but interdependent.

For our part we bishops cannot imagine ourselves entering a new millennium, embarked upon a new evangelization, unless we walk side by side with our lay sisters and brothers. For together we stand at the threshold of a "great venture, both challenging and wonderful . . . re-evangelization so much needed by the present world" (*Christifideles Laici*, no. 64).

Reflecting on the last fifteen years, we see how much we have to be grateful for in the lives and witness of the lay faithful. Looking ahead, we envision what might be. For the vision to take flesh, however, we need to commit ourselves anew, bishops and people, to prayer and dialogue, to reflection and action.

Discussion Questions

1. Do you think there has been a greater maturing of Catholic laity in the past fifteen years? How has this been manifested?
2. As an adult Catholic, how do you keep growing in the faith—spiritually and intellectually?
3. What do you consider the most important responsibility of a Catholic Christian adult in our society today?
4. Have you experienced yourself as a partner with the hierarchy in church life and mission? What have you learned from this experience?

Selected Additional Resources

These documents are available from USCCB Publishing, United States Conference of Catholic Bishops, 3211 Fourth St., N.E., Washington, DC 20017; 1-800-235-8722.

United States Conference of Catholic Bishops. *Follow the Way of Love*. 1993. Publication No. 7-240 (English). Available in e-book format only. A pastoral message to families, written in readable style, which offers support and encourages mutuality in marriage roles.

United States Conference of Catholic Bishops. *Go and Make Disciples/Tenth Anniversary Edition*. 2002. Publication No. 5-475 (Bilingual). National plan and strategy for Catholic evangelization in the United States.

Catechism of the Catholic Church (Second Edition). Publication No. 5-110 (English paperback), 7-205 (English e-book), 5-844 (Spanish hardback), 5-828 (Spanish paperback), and 7-829 (Spanish e-book). Primary references to the lay faithful may be found in the following paragraphs: 873-875, 897-913, 928-929. Secondary references may be found in the following paragraphs: 784-786, 863, 1268, 2044, 2105, 2442, 2472.

United States Conference of Catholic Bishops. *Stewardship: A Disciple's Response/Tenth Anniversary Edition*. 2003. Publication No. 5-465 (English), 5-465e (English e-book), and 5-883 (Spanish). Pastoral message to all Catholics, presenting stewardship as an expression of discipleship.

Pope John Paul II. *The Gospel of Life/Evangelium Vitae*. 1995. Publication No. 316-7 (English) and 317-5 (Spanish). Encyclical letter on the legal, moral, and ethical threats to life.

United States Conference of Catholic Bishops. *A Decade After Economic Justice for All: Constant Principles, Changing Context, Continuing Challenges*. 1995. Publication No. 5-040 (English). The bishops' reflections on the economy, particularly in light of the 1986 pastoral letter *Economic Justice for All*.

United States Conference of Catholic Bishops. *Strengthening the Bonds of Peace*. 1994. Available online at *usccb.org* (search for the resource title). A pastoral reflection on women and their roles in Church and in society.

Resources on Lay Ministry

These documents are available from USCCB Publishing, United States Conference of Catholic Bishops, 3211 Fourth Street, N.E., Washington, DC, 20017; 1-800-235-8722.

Co-Workers in the Vineyard of the Lord: A Resource for Guiding the Development of Lay Ecclesial Ministry. 2006. Publication No. 5-724. Offers pastoral and theological reflections on the reality of lay ecclesial ministry, affirmation of those who serve in this way, and a synthesis of best thinking and practice. It is a resource for diocesan bishops and for all others who are responsible for guiding the development of lay ecclesial ministry in the United States.

Lay Ecclesial Ministry: The State of the Questions. 2000. Publication No. 5-345 (English) and 5-864 (Spanish). Presents a summary of the "Leadership for Ecclesial Lay Ministry" project and invites the bishops to determine the future course of the project in order to serve the need for leadership at the national level and provide practical assistance at the local level.

Together in God's Service: Toward a Theology of Ecclesial Lay Ministry. 1998. Publication No. 5-285. Explores the theological basis for the growing phenomenon of "lay ecclesial minister" as well as the sociological and demographic reality of such ministers. Also probes the sacramental theology, church history, Scripture, canon law, and magisterial teaching to help explain a lay ecclesial minister's place in the life of the Church.